Learning to Drive Nails

by Dwaine Spieker

Rogue Faculty Press
Omaha, Nebraska

Copyright©2018 by Dwaine Spieker
ISBN 978-0-692-14576-0

First Edition

Cover art by Calvin Banks
Author photo by Mollie Spieker

The author is grateful to the following publications, where some of these poems first appeared: *Plainsongs*, *Nimrod*, and *Aethlon*.

Printed in the USA on acid-free paper.
To order online, go to *amazon.com*

Contents

For my children.

Songbirds

Who can blame them
for thinking it's spring?

It's late January
and fifty-seven degrees.

Who can blame them
for being so confident

that winter is over?
For thinking they know

more than they do?
For feeling so old,

or old enough,
and edging out to

the song-tip of youth?

Spring Song

We walk
in song
all spring.

We walk
in spring,
all song.

We walk,
spring song
in all,

in all.

A Week of Rain

Too many droughts
   lie in my past
for me to refuse
   all this excess.

Too many dry seasons
   wait in my future
for me to complain
   of all this water.

Too much hard rain
   may now be present,
but life is too arid,
   too unlike this moment

to wish this moisture
   would gradually end,
or suddenly stop,
   or, even less, lessen.

Old Water Heater

No doubt replaced
by a better model,
much more efficient
with smaller capacity,
it stands near the curb
of its former house,
free for the taking,
like the body of a rocket
that has fallen back,
spent, to a sea of grass.
Except it is standing
up on its end, as if
still aimed at the heavens,
holding the spacecraft
of obsolete technology
and its rover of loss,
counting down seconds
to some kind of liftoff.

Learning to Drive Nails

The wood a scrap two-by-four
   caked with dried cement,
the nails new ten-pennies
   lifted from his father's workbench;

the time late July, the heat
   late-afternoon intense;
the scene an apple orchard near
   a tractorless quonset;

the handle hickory, by and for
   the leveraged hands of men,
gripped too loose, swung too high;
   the frustrated clawhead

turns nail after nail aside
   bruised, blistered, bent.
The boy's hands cry, throb,
   painfully grow accurate.

Great Grandmother

Beaded by arthritis,
her knuckles and joints
were a rosary of pain
she never stopped praying.

Welder

He set his clamps,
checked his ground.

Then, lowering his helmet,
he closed his arc,

himself the bead
between worlds.

Headstones (I)

Not one marker here is the size nor shape
of a skipping stone, yet the mind
wishes to curl one in its forefinger
and whip it sidearm, over the surface

of the great mystery. Still others strike
the spirit as spherical, beg to be hurled
overhand as far out into the deep
as one's power allows. Irresistible,

this urge to test one's skill and strength
against these stones, sidelong or overhand,
tricking a few skips out of physics
or making the most distant splash one can.

On a Clear Afternoon

Each headstone
is a pair of bifocals:

the infinitely distant
and the local.

The Dead

In stone tuxedos
and marble dresses,

they wear flowers,
a wedding party.

As today this life
marries the next,

they have little to do
except be beautiful,

the witnesses.

Nightcrawlers

This morning's rain is strong and warm,
a heavy rain of nostalgia, not the past
as it actually happened, but that story
you tell yourself as you make sense

of what happened. So calm, but there,
there come the worms that always emerge
and lie on the pavement, waterlogged.
Sometimes this happens when rain falls:

you recall things you never meant
to see again, and there they sprawl,
soaked and stranded, out of their element.
You wish for a way to help them along.

Moving a Barn

Do not swerve
or brake hard.
Keep the truck
in low gear,

do not speed,
but dammit,
don't dilly-
dally either.

Watch out for
loose gravel
as you turn
corners. And

don't—do not—
think too much.
Forget what
you're doing

but keep on
doing it,
unlikely
as it is.

Nest

A robin this spring has built her nest
over our doorway. Oddly enough,
she's hung it from a decorative nub
atop the light fixture, looped there
with one dry shaft of fountain grass.
It's a well-woven home, shaded,
prosperous—quite an accomplishment.
But think if your home were suspended
by a lone blade of grass, one strand
holding everything you've worked for
not just this spring but all your years.
There it is, all you have woven,
between a scorching porchlight
and a wobbly awning, dangling
from a decorative nub: all your success.
Well, that's how it is for this robin.

Vinyl Flowers

The problems with real flowers
led to their invention.

More durable and permanent
than actual lilies or daffodils,

they are just as beautiful
at a distance. Not as precious,

they hold up stronger in sun,
better resist wind,

and more fully resemble
our losses, our grief.

Sometimes you will find them
blown miles from any cemetery,

hidden in weedy ditches,
dirty, a bit frayed and faded,

still blooming.

To a Substitute Teacher

Now it is your absence
we struggle to fill

since that moment you covered
for each of us.

Monday Morning

and the town cemetery
is a kind of cafe,

a small diner
with a bay window

where the local dead
gather for coffee.

As everyone else
is rushing to work,

their lives sealed
tight as thermoses

or travel mugs,
here the dead

linger and sip
from open cups,

the faint steam
of what they were

rising into their talk.

Photosynthesis

The town swimming pool
is a blue leaf,

converting afternoon light
into children.

To Our Unborn Child

In the fog, our streetlamp
is a womb of soft light,
a glow the same hue

as the ultrasound image
we saw of you today—
today, late afternoon.

It's as if you are walking
toward us through fog
and soft orange light,

a stranger who needs shelter
from the mist and the night.
Welcome, son. Come inside.

Swordplay

At his behest,   I've hewn a sword
out of a pine   one-by-four
for my eight-year-old.   I barely had
the edges sanded   before he grabbed it
and ran off to battle   in the alfalfa field
west of our house.
                              Now he is showing
surprising skill   at swordsmanship,
slaying an onslaught   of ominous ogres
single-handed.
                         Here there is no more
actual death   than in those fantasies
and comic books   he loves so much
he's memorized their moves.   Beyond the hill
the last light   lances the clouds
and only the sunset   bleeds red.

Quarter to Six on Tuesday

Someone is up running a chainsaw
already this morning. Across town
arrives the high hum of the blade
bearing down, easing off,
and bearing down hard again.
Surprising to hear a revving saw
so early, but no surprise at all
to think of another long workday
easing off late last evening
and a new one chainsawing down
now over the next few hours.
Through it all is the revving rhythm
of the working life, its high hum
rising and spreading over town.

Corpus Christi Sunday Afternoon

The slow shadow of a lone cloud
tablecloths the local cemetery,
and on its cotton the dead spread out
their parish picnic, a moveable feast.

Baskets of bread, decanters of wine,
block after block of good cheese.
Adults laugh and dance to accordions
as children play tag in the breeze.

Then the cloud slips off to the east,
taking all but the dead's hospitality.
In sunlight again, you remember the scene,
the way the dead smiled and were waving.

Auto-Parts Store

Like a library, its shelves are packed,
not only with battery chargers
and metric wrenches, but with narratives
of other lives you might have led.

Weekend mechanic or full-time,
outlaw hot-rodder, aficionado
of classic models, motorcyclist,
or parts man for this very store—

each life shows its spine and title.
Walking by the windshield wipers
is like passing through Biographies.
No way could you read them all.

Junkyard for Combines

Old Gleaners and John Deeres,
Internationals and Allises,
with wide heads on enormous shoulders

they look like bison, seeming to graze
tall roadside grass this afternoon,
browning with rust in light and wind.

Somewhere overhead, a satellite
passes like a miniscule sun,
guiding the newer implements

like Manifest Destiny. Yet in their prime
these harvesters were all range animals,
rugged creatures, part of a species

who did not need a signal stronger
than their own strength to roam the hills,
nor any data but their own ability

to cover ground. These individuals'
time may be past, their roving over,
but clearly the breed is integral

to the environment, their kind vital
to freedom's complex ecosystem.
It must not be allowed to go extinct.

True Story

It landed here by accident,
a single Nike hiking boot,
twelve miles south of Wayne, Nebraska,
along Highway 15, east shoulder,
pointing straight west. Here
it has remained for over a year,
still standing, surviving traffic,
multiple snows and snowplows,
all weathers, countless gusts.
Right now it is even outlasting
some passerby's recent attempt
to pretty it up, filling it with
an old bouquet of vinyl flowers.
Not even this is too much.

Hammock

So easy on a summer afternoon
to sprawl out on the big hammock
of the past, and lie there a while,
hands as a pillow, swinging and swinging.

And even easier, so comfortable,
to fall asleep there, and easier still
to start that dream of your personal past
that is and is not real memory.

For summer days are not the time
for the hard work of remembering things
exactly as they happened. Easiest of all
is waking again, refreshed by the story.

July

When the past
tassels

and pollinates
each silk of memory.

Alfalfa Field

The westbound windrows run back
into the past,

and the eastbound windrows
run back with some kind of memory.

On this bright and breezy afternoon
they run back and run back,

west and east and west again,
motionless and all motion.

Pitchfork

It taught me early how much weight
a forkful was, the right amount
of rye straw or prairie hay
to pitch forward or lift over
without laziness or overstrain.
Footing. Poise. Balance. Shape.
The right amount, held eye-level,
hung to my waist, strangely buoyant.

My right hand ran the handle;
the clumsier left served as fulcrum
and bore the load. It taught me early
how good work felt, how cleaning up
and clearing out approached perfection,
how fork by fork I could heft tons.

Northwest of Elgin

The cows and calves of loss
are pasturing on the sandhills
of my life, grazing it down
mouthful by mouthful.

For luck,
my spring saw plentiful rain.
July and grass is still thick,
still moist, still green.

But today, a dry wind
touches each shortening blade.
Even the grass is finite,
even long summers fade.

FM

On the radio
of this warm afternoon

play the pop songs
of nostalgia.

How simplistic
their music and lyrics,

but how sophisticated
the signal,

the circuitry,
the actual

electronics!

Walking

Wherever
you are,

you are
halfway.

Halfway
already.

Already
and only,

walking.

Swim-Meet Timer

Stopwatch up, I click it on
at the starter's whistle. A few drops
of the swimmer's push-off splash my legs.

Already she's far gone, halfway down
into her backstroke. A moment here
to check my clipboard—Heat Two, Lane One,

Girls' Twelve-to-Fourteen Division.
A moment here to watch her arms
fan back and back away from me,

her breathing calm, enviably measured,
a well-coached kid with good technique,
back and back into the cooling sun.

A moment here to let my stopwatch
hang at my chest, a chance to scan
the crowd outside the chain-link fence,

the trees and park, the speeding sun.
All of us are backstroking fast
into the second half of another year,

kicking hard under the blue surface
of life in time. We're so well-coached.
My Lane-One swimmer executes

an expert turn—more good technique.
A moment yet to hold this scene
as firmly as I hold this clipboard

and now my clock. She's halfway home,
and those drops she splashed up on my legs
are drying fast. Watch, *stop.*

Wheeler County, Nebraska
—in memory of my grandfather

The Cattle of the Sun God
pastured on hills like these,

but out here you can be Odysseus
without the crew in mutiny.

When your Ithaca and your Great Sea
are one,

when Helios and Poseidon and Aeolus
are not your enemies,

you can have the epic hero's scope
without his suffering.

Smartphone

The man slides it out of his breast pocket
like a pack of cigarettes, as his grandfather did
his Lucky Strikes, and with that exact
unthinkingness thumbs the passcode.

Just as his ancestor would cup hands
around the match and its precious flame,
he holds this phone and all its icons,
its background screen, its Otter case.

The first inhale was what tasted best
to the old smoker. Into this bloodstream
flows the nicotine of iMessages.
The pale light. A face relieved.

Sunset in July

The days are still hot and long,
but already shorter each night.
We will have to grow more diligent

about our labor, more dedicated
even to our rest and slow leisure.
We'll have to make do with less light.

Son

At preschool you have learned to sing
 the Happy Birthday song
to time how long to wash your hands
 to make sure germs are gone.

And so at only three years old
 you've sung that little tune
more times than I, your father, have
 at over forty-two.

Son, all those years have taught me how
 the world can stain your hands.
And no song, sad to say, can wash
 your soul and flesh pure again.

May all your birthdays be like this
 and all the years between:
free of the filth of life, or made
 by living water clean.

Old Puzzles and Games in the Basement

After so many years of never being
put away right, they now fill up
an oversized Rubbermaid container,

mixed, compounded, complicated,
thousands and thousands of pieces,
a dozen sets of different rules.

Each set was once a thorough vision,
an image or a game, an arrangement
that would have fit or played so well,

but here their pieces are, all as one,
the way life sometimes turns out,
pieces of old futures mixed together.

Black 1967 Mustang Cobra

A car that made you Jupiter:
a 428 of pure omnipotence
with glasspack thunderbolts,
it rent the sky and earth
and outran Mercury in quarters.

The nymphs that fastback knew!
A car for overthrowing fathers.
On Friday nights, the trunk a cask
of Bacchus Lite, subwoofers harping
AC/DC as you cruised Olympus,

or west of town, when it was floored,
your aegis a speedometer that read
one hundred forty miles per hour—
my God! It could have been
your chariot to immortality.

Pulling Tractor

Like so many others here at the fair,
this International 966
came of age working the farm,

yet now with oversized back tires
and custom graphics, chrome stack
and monster engine, it cannot return.

As its field work or daily chores,
it hooks to a sled that bears down
harder the longer it's pulled forward,

like leaving the farm. The torque and roar,
the strength and smoke of its exhibitions
exhaust that loss, over and over.

Elegy in August

August is always
part of the past.

With cornfields
at black-green

and cicadas at song,
it is a fullness

we cannot hold
except in memory,

a present abundance
we cannot abide

until it retires
into personal history.

We are part spring,
part harvest,

and mostly winter.
Summer eludes us,

year after year.

Tantalus

As Teacher
>He stands to his neck
>>in a calm lake of papers.
>He earned his way here.

As Reader
>The more he squints down
>>at the book, hunching his back,
>the page disappears.

As Poet
>Under trees laden
>>with what is untouchable,
>he still reaches up.

Late Summer

On the tallest diving board
stands a high-school boy,
not gripping the rails.

Tight as baseball leather
are his biceps and pecs,
and big as haybales.

Shouting at the lifeguard,
he runs and jumps.
His leap is not yet a fall.

State Baseball Championship Banner

Not nearly as large as a movie screen,
it hangs downtown, but painted on its plywood
the names of players, coaches, and managers
read like credits of a motion picture.

Looking up on this summer afternoon,
you feel like a latecomer who's arrived
at what was once a crowded theater,
the feature of that season long since over.

What the story was, what performances
helped bring home this Academy Award,
you can't tell from the sign alone.
You'd have to ask around to find out.

Wide Receiver, Broken Play

Our quarterback scrambling right
and my own passing route broken,
I doubled back, found open ground,
and waved my arms. Off-balance,
he lobbed a wobbly pass my direction,
and I leapt to catch it two-handed
high over my helmet. First Down.

I thought of that play this morning,
now that my chronic back problems
have subsided again. Briefly, for now,
I've shaken off the cornerback
of middle age and stand wide open,
the wobbly pass of a pain-free day
lobbed my direction. First Down.

Error

Bunt back to pitcher. . . .
After fastballs all summer,
he overthrows first.

Stainless Steel

Pinned to the fabric of this maple
is a Butterick pattern of leaves,
and now would be the perfect time

for my mother's sewing scissors,
the all-steel pair she kept
polished with a scrap of corduroy

and hidden in the back of that drawer.
Now that I'm older, perhaps
I could be trusted to cut out

one crackling piece of fall
with those unfingerprinted Fiskars?
I promise, promise I'll be careful.

Golden Harvest

As dementia
tasseled like a cornfield
inside his head,

he wandered in
and like a child got lost
among its stalks,

which without rows
stood like no other crop
he ever planted.

Junk Sofa

Twisted, legless, ripped, bleached from exposure,
it rests atop a pile of brush and branches
like an abandoned canoe on a sandbar.
Someday soon, after a good, hard rain,
the river of fire will rise beneath its hull
and on a quickened current float it away.

September Night

Cicadas ride
their rusty bikes,

crickets skateboards
or red wagons,

and everyone else
some kind of scooter

as tonight we all
wheel toward autumn,

our going slow
and self-propelled.

Always in September

Crickets clink like coffee mugs,
making these dark September mornings
church-basement tables, where sit
so many men, long since gone.

There's Leo Schindler, farming accident;
Merle Schmitt, dropped at forty by
a brain aneurysm; and Bill Beckman,
whose giant body outlived his mind

by twenty years. So many others,
the men who were the men of town
I still look up to. Always in September
they gather again, sipping the darkness.

Farm-Store Advertising Flyer

Sweatshirts are on sale, flannels
and fleeces, barncoats and coveralls,
and for the first time snowboots,

a sure sign. It's late October,
the clothes have all changed colors,
and even your mailbox is a sky

you watch for signs of cold weather.
Everything portends the big change
we all know is coming, but when

is so uncertain. Even this flyer
is a paper goose, migrating through,
its wings spread wide on your table.

After Harvest

The trees take off
their work caps

and with a slow, gray
lather of weather

wash their forearms,
their hands.

The First Sunday in November

All summer, even our local dead
abided by Daylight Savings Time,
and today they like all of us
adjust again in time for winter.

As we living reset our clocks,
the dead themselves fall back
to our time, the time of this life,
when one hour is so precious,

but of course they can spring forward
whenever they wish, to life beyond time,
look back at us with pity and love,
click shut and repocket their watches.

Ulysses, Nebraska

The old rail cuts the town in half.

* *

For fifty years the cars would load with corn,
seal their lids, and move on,

past the elevator, between the hayfields,
beyond the Platte river.

* *

After that,
the burrs snarled up in the gravel
and bit the heads off the spikes.

* *

Trains took the town's grain. And never came back.

Pill Bottles

Our bathroom cabinet is filled
with these shotgun shells.

With them we hunt the ringneck
pheasants of health.

Or at least its turtledoves and quail.

We load our bodies like guns,
look out at November.

And walk out into the tall brown grass
of its fields.

Electric Fence

Tonight the constellations are all cattle
grazing the sandhills of outer space,
and keeping them herded together afield
is an electric fence, a single wire
through which ticks a current of meaning.

Of course it's a trick; of course they could trample
the fence in an instant, the shock so small
compared to their strength, size, and girth.
But the stars stay away, and the fence stands
thin but distinct. Somehow it works.

Owl

The past is a nocturnal bird,
resting in some leafless tree
back up over your shoulder.

Often, waking before dawn,
you can hear the old creature
call from wherever it's hidden,

clawed hard to the darkness.
You walk into the day, the owl
behind you everywhere and noplace.

Trying on Frames

Because I am so nearsighted
when it comes to fashion, I need
my wife to help me choose
new eyeglass frames. Pair
after pair after pair I try on
at her behest, before they go
into the big pile of NO
or the small stack of YES.

Then it's a small tournament
of plastic and wire, us pausing,
me turning side to side,
her fussing over me. I love her help
in how I see, what I choose,
how I look to the world. I do.

Power Outage

—for my children

That night when a hard winter wind
darkened the house,
I moved from room to room
to steady your skiffs of sleep
and re-tuck in each of you.

I brought along
only the calmest possible breeze,
a flashlight beam,
a took care even that
did not visit your faces too roughly.

My children, when I am gone,
please know that for one night at least
your father had power
to calm winds and still waters.

Headstones (II)

Many could be taken
for small fireplaces,

hearths that still
glow with warmth.

Thus people come,
redden the embers

with vinyl flowers,
and to the new flames

offer their hands.

Thunderbird

November, and this wind is blowing me back
to the past, back to the driver's seat
of my high-school car, and I am speeding to town
for predawn basketball practice.

November has felt like preseason since,
the near future as outstretched and open
as the widespread wings on that hood ornament.

Splitting Firewood

At some point
one must stop
thinking simply
of the present.

At some point
this or any
one moment
grows inadequate.

At some point
time tips forward,
life leans
toward the future,

and only preparation
for next season
verifies an instant.
At some point,

and we passed it.

Wish

That this cold spell has found
everyone I have ever wronged,

and brought each one of them inside
somewhere warm, if not at home.

That there there's a lit fireplace
or good furnace, the right light,

enough laughter to foster forgiveness,
and for each, the drink of choice.

About the Author

Dwaine Spieker teaches British Literature, Composition, and Creative Writing at Wayne High School in Wayne, Nebraska. After growing up on a farm outside Elgin, Nebraska, he attended the University of Nebraska at Kearney, graduating in 1997, and received his MA from the University of Nebraska-Lincoln in 2001. Spieker has been the recipient of National Endowment for the Humanities grants in the Summer Seminars for School Teachers program twice (2002 and 2007), and in 2009 the Wayne Area Economic Development Council named him Educator of the Year.

Spieker's poetry has appeared in *Plainsongs, The Platte Valley Review, The Nebraska Poets Calendar, The Plain Song Review, The Omaha World-Herald, Nebraska Life, Midwest Quarterly, Aethlon, Nimrod,* and *Prairie Schooner*. His first book, *Garden of Stars*, published by All Along Press of St. Louis, MO, won the 2010 Nebraska Book Award for Poetry. His second collection, *The Way Magellan Must Have Felt*, was published by Rogue Faculty Press in 2014. He was also a finalist for the 2014 Pablo Neruda Prize from *Nimrod* and a semi-finalist in 2015. Recently he edited *Homing: The Collected Poems of Don Welch, 1975-2015*, published by Rogue Faculty Press in 2016, which also won the Nebraska Book Award.

Beginning in March 2019, he will serve as the poetry editor for *Nebraska Life* Magazine.

Spieker lives in Wayne with his four children.

Acknowledgments

The author would like to thank Kael Sagheer for her optimism despite encountering the book in manuscript. Jeff Lacey and Calvin Banks of Rogue Faculty Press continue to encourage him in poetry and the art of motorcycle maintenance.

The author's children, to whom this book is dedicated, know the strange boy in the title poem as a full-grown man. His parents and siblings have known him as both a boy and man–and seem to love him anyway.

Finally, the author also would like the reader to know that laser-corrective eye surgery is but one reason he no longer tries on eyeglass frames.